PRESENT
not perfect

A JOURNAL FOR
SLOWING DOWN, LETTING GO,
AND LOVING WHO YOU ARE

Aimee Chase,
author of *One Question a Day*

CASTLE POINT BOOKS
NEW YORK

www.stmartins.com
www.castlepointbooks.com

The Castle Point Books trademark is owned
by Castle Point Publications, LLC.
Castle Point books are published and
distributed by St. Martin's Press.

ISBN 978-1-250-14775-2 (trade paperback)

Cover design by Katie Jennings Campbell
Interior design by Katie Jennings Campbell and Tara Long

Images used under license from Shutterstock.com

Our books may be purchased in bulk for promotional, educational,
or business use. Please contact your local bookseller or the
Macmillan Corporate and Premium Sales Department
at 1-800-221-7945, extension 5442, or by e-mail
at MacmillanSpecialMarkets@macmillan.com.

First Edition: September 2017

10 9 8 7 6 5 4 3 2

THIS JOURNAL BELONGS <u>TO</u>

THE ARTIST WHO
AIMS FOR
PERFECTION
IN EVERYTHING
ACHIEVES IT
IN NOTHING.
—EUGENE DELACROIX

INTRODUCTION

THINK OF ALL THE MOMENTS you spend critiquing yourself, your life, or others because they fall short of perfection. Those are joyless moments. Imagine that, instead of allowing your inner voice to deplete your joy, you could train it to find wonder and satisfaction every day.

Present, not Perfect is an artful, creative approach to daily mindfulness. Each page features a simple exercise or a lighthearted quote to help you feel more present in the moment and awaken a sense of gratitude and strength.

Use this journal as a quiet refuge from stress and negativity. Find the pages that move you and fill them with your honest thoughts and feelings. Free yourself from the dizzying pursuit of perfection and embrace the charming disarray of your real and fabulously-flawed life.

Surrender to the moment

BY OBSERVING ALL THAT IS HAPPENING IN AND AROUND YOU.

WRITE DOWN ALL THE SOUNDS YOU CAN HEAR RIGHT NOW:

WHAT SCENTS DO YOU NOTICE, IF ANY?

WRITE DOWN (IN BRIGHT COLORED PENS)
3 THINGS *that bring you joy.*

1.

2.

3.

WRITE DOWN (IN PENCIL) 3 THINGS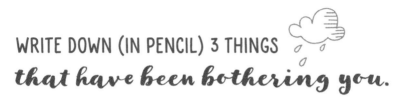
that have been bothering you.

1.

2.

3.

ERASE THE ITEMS ON THE SECOND LIST OVER WHICH YOU DO NOT HAVE
TOTAL CONTROL. AS YOU GENTLY BLOW THE RESIDUE OFF OF THE PAGE,
IMAGINE THAT YOU ARE RELEASING YOUR WORRIES. SAY TO YOURSELF:

COME WHAT MAY.

YOU
WERE BORN
TO BE

REAL
NOT TO BE

PERFECT.

Close your eyes
and try to quiet
your mind for one
full minute.

IMAGINE THE STATIC OF YOUR THOUGHTS
GETTING QUIETER AND QUIETER.

WHICH THOUGHTS, IF ANY, DID YOU
HAVE TROUBLE QUIETING JUST THEN?

THINK OF YOUR LIFE AS A SCRAPBOOK OF EXPERIENCES.

WHAT IMAGE WOULD YOU PLACE IN THE SCRAPBOOK TODAY?

WHAT DOES THIS IMAGE SAY ABOUT YOUR DAY AND HOW YOU FEEL ABOUT IT?

WHAT DOES THIS IMAGE SAY ABOUT YOU?

CIRCLE YOUR FAVORITE ITEMS FROM THIS LIST OF BEAUTIFULLY IMPERFECT THINGS

A WRINKLED NOTE FROM AN OLD FRIEND

AN AWKWARD FIRST KISS

SEA GLASS

A CHILD'S DRAWING

A WORN BUT WELL-LOVED BOOK

AN UN-POSED FAMILY PORTRAIT

ADD MORE BEAUTIFULLY IMPERFECT ITEMS HERE:

GLUE OR TAPE A FAVORITE
PHOTOGRAPH OF YOURSELF HERE

DESCRIBE WHAT YOU LIKE ABOUT THIS PHOTO.

WHAT ARE ALL OF THE THINGS YOU'RE TRYING TO (OR TRIED TO) GET DONE TODAY?

Write them between the overlapping shapes below.

WHAT TASK OR ACCOMPLISHMENTS WILL LEAVE YOU FEELING MOST FULFILLED AT THE END OF THIS DAY?

WRITE IT IN THE CENTER OF THE CIRCLE ABOVE.
RESOLVE TO DO IT PURPOSEFULLY RATHER THAN QUICKLY.

GIVE THIS ACTION ITS OWN
MOMENT IN TIME.

WHAT ARE YOUR FAVORITE
SENSORY-RICH FOODS?

Use them to help you press pause during a busy day.

CIRCLE YOUR FAVORITES FROM THESE OPTIONS OR ADD YOUR OWN:

HARD CANDY

CHOCOLATE

BREATH MINT

HOT TEA

SLOW DOWN AND EAT MINDFULLY TODAY.
Savor the first three bites of every food you eat.
Notice the food's texture, temperature, and flavor,
what it brings to mind, and what feelings it inspires.
Record your observations here:

FOOD 1:

FOOD 2:

FOOD 3:

GIVE YOURSELF PERMISSION TO BE

HAPPY

EVERY DAY

SURPRISE YOURSELF TODAY.

Instead of feeling swept along by a frenzied schedule,
stop to do one thing you didn't expect to have time to do.

CHOOSE ONE OF THESE OPTIONS IF YOU NEED INSPIRATION:

1. email an old friend

2. take a joy ride

3. call in sick

4. make conversation with someone new

5. sign up for a class

6. make something by hand

7. frame a favorite old photo

8. plan a weekend getaway

GIVE YOURSELF TIME TODAY

TO STARE OUT THE CLOSEST WINDOW AT SOMETHING
BEAUTIFUL. IMAGINE THAT YOUR BRAIN IS GETTING OFF
THE HIGHWAY TO ENJOY A MORE SCENIC SIDE ROAD.

WHAT EMOTIONS AND THOUGHTS
FLOAT TO THE SURFACE WHEN YOU
REMOVE DISTRACTIONS?

WHAT PART OF YOUR DAY LENDS ITSELF
BEST TO TAKING A SCREEN BREAK?

WRITE DOWN THREE FEARS THAT HOLD YOU BACK.

1.

2.

3.

IMAGINE PLACING THEM INSIDE OF THESE
HOT-AIR BALLOONS AND WATCHING THEM
DRIFT AWAY. WHAT WOULD YOU BE FREE TO DO?

LOOK AT THE PAINT COLORS BELOW AND CHOOSE THE ONE THAT BEST DEFINES YOUR MOOD TODAY.

Circle the color and notice how you feel when you look at it. Accept whatever mood you are in, but give it a name below:

_____

WHAT ALWAYS IMPROVES YOUR MOOD WHEN YOU'RE HAVING A GOOD DAY?

WHAT HAS THE POWER TO DARKEN YOUR MOOD WHEN YOU'RE HAVING A GREAT DAY?

HOW CAN YOU MINIMIZE ITS INFLUENCE ON YOU?

MAKING
MISTAKES IS
BETTER THAN
FAKING
PERFECTIONS

THINK OF ONE MISTAKE YOU'VE MADE RECENTLY,
NO MATTER HOW BIG OR SMALL,
AND WRITE ABOUT IT BELOW:

WRITE WHY IT'S NOT SUCH A BIG DEAL AFTER ALL OR HOW
SOMETHING GOOD MIGHT COME OF IT:

CONSIDER ALL THE PEOPLE WHO
WILL **LOVE** YOU NO
MATTER HOW MANY
MISTAKES YOU MAKE.
WRITE THEIR NAMES HERE:

TAKE A MINUTE TO CHOOSE YOUR OWN SPIRIT-ROUSING MANTRA.
NEED HELP? THINK OF THE WORDS THAT YOU WISH SOMEONE
WOULD SAY TO YOU EACH AND EVERY DAY.

Consider these choices or create your own:

I've got this.

I am the sky. Everything else is the weather.

I am incredible.

Perfection is overrated.

WRITE YOUR FAVORITE MANTRA ON THE BANNER TO THE RIGHT.
CONSIDER POSTING IT NEAR YOUR FRONT DOOR SO THAT YOU CAN READ IT
BEFORE YOU LEAVE EVERY DAY FOR A DAILY DOSE OF INSPIRATION.

RELEASE YOURSELF FROM THE TIRING PURSUIT OF UNREALISTIC GOALS.

START BY IDENTIFYING YOUR GOALS AS UNREALISTIC OR REALISTIC.

UNREALISTIC GOALS
⬇

REALISTIC GOALS
⬇

HOW COULD YOU SOFTEN SOME OF THE UNREALISTIC GOALS
TO MAKE THEM EASIER TO ACHIEVE?

CHOOSE ONE WAY TO
revisit your childhood today
AND REFLECT ON HOW FAR YOU'VE COME.

- [ ] DRIVE BY YOUR CHILDHOOD HOME

- [ ] LISTEN TO A SONG YOU LOVED AS A KID

- [ ] CALL OR SEND A MESSAGE TO
  AN OLD FRIEND OR FAMILY MEMBER

- [ ] WATCH A HOME VIDEO

- [ ] FLIP THROUGH OLD PHOTOS

LIST 3 WAYS THAT YOU HAVE GROWN AS A PERSON:

1.

2.

3.

IDENTIFY AN AREA OF STRENGTH BELOW:

romance

WORK

PHYSICAL
HEALTH

FRIENDSHIP

WHICH AREA COULD YOU REDEFINE FOR YOURSELF SO THAT
YOU FEEL MORE SATISFIED?

TAKE COMFORT IN THE NOTION
THAT EVERYTHING FEELS LESS IMPORTANT
WITH A LITTLE TIME OR DISTANCE.

Imagine that you are looking back at your life
from a ripe old age, or looking down at your life from
a million miles away.

WHAT WOULD MATTER
MOST FROM THIS PERSPECTIVE?

WHAT WOULD SEEM SMALL AND INCONSEQUENTIAL
FROM THIS PERSPECTIVE?

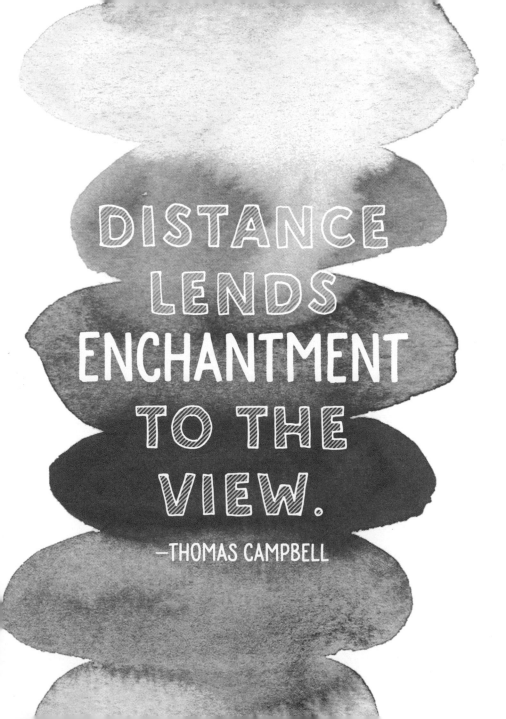

DISTANCE LENDS ENCHANTMENT TO THE VIEW.

—THOMAS CAMPBELL

CONSIDER THE WAYS IN WHICH
YOU MAKE OTHER PEOPLES' LIVES EASIER OR BETTER.

IT CAN BE ANYTHING FROM OPENING DOORS FOR STRANGERS
TO LENDING AN EAR WHEN A FRIEND NEEDS IT.

LIST ALL THAT YOU DO HERE:

WHO ARE THE PEOPLE THAT VALUE THE ROLE
YOU PLAY IN THEIR LIVES?

Friendship
ISN'T A BIG THING.
IT'S A MILLION
LITTLE THINGS.

WHAT ARE THE THEMES OF YOUR LIFE? WHAT PATTERNS DO YOU
EXPERIENCE IN YOUR RELATIONSHIPS OR LIFE EXPERIENCES?
MAYBE YOU DRAW PEOPLE TO YOU, GET BURNT OUT FROM TRYING TOO HARD,
HAVE REALLY GOOD LUCK, OR MAKE MOUNTAINS OUT OF MOLEHILLS.

WRITE THEM IN THE WHITE WAVES BELOW.
Accept them and let them flow.

LOOK FOR SOMETHING BEAUTIFUL
THAT YOU MIGHT HAVE BEEN IGNORING
UP UNTIL THIS MOMENT.
Describe its beauty here:

IMAGINE SOMEONE IS DESCRIBING *YOUR* BEAUTY.
Write their description below.

If you like what you've written,
place it on your refrigerator or
your bathroom mirror.

TAKE A FEW BREATHS TO FILL YOURSELF WITH
hope, positivity, and lightness.

IMAGINE THAT AS YOU INHALE, YOU
ARE DRAWING GOLDEN LIGHT INTO YOUR BODY.

AS YOU EXHALE, YOU ARE EXPELLING ALL
OF YOUR WORRIES AND NEGATIVE FEELINGS.

REPEAT THIS PROCESS UNTIL YOU
feel lighter and more relaxed.

THINK OF YOUR FAVORITE SONG.

HUM IT QUIETLY TO YOURSELF OR BELT IT OUT. NOTICE THE LYRICS.
WHICH WORDS SPEAK TO YOU MOST?
WRITE THEM HERE:

MAKE A LIST OF OTHER SONGS
THAT MAKE YOU HAPPY. WRITE THEM BELOW AND
PLAY THEM FOR YOURSELF TODAY.

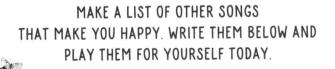

TIME SEEMS TO PASS TOO QUICKLY.
STOP TO TAKE A "SNAPSHOT"
OF THIS MOMENT.

DESCRIBE WHAT'S HAPPENING WITHIN YOU
AND AROUND YOU:

WHAT DO YOU WANT TO REMEMBER MOST
ABOUT THIS MOMENT?

CLOSE YOUR EYES AND MAKE A WISH:

WHY DO YOU NEED THIS WISH TO COME TRUE?

WHY DON'T YOU NEED THIS WISH TO COME TRUE?

USE A MORNING RITUAL TO FEEL MORE PRESENT.

Practice turning a mindless activity into a mindful, sensory experience:

wash your hands

brush your teeth

blow dry your hair

make your bed

How do the bristles of your toothbrush feel against your teeth? How does the cold rush of water feel against your hands? If your mind rushes ahead, where does it want to go? Describe your experience here:

THE TIME TO
BE HAPPY IS NOW.
THE PLACE TO BE
HAPPY IS HERE.

—Robert Green Ingersoll

LET YOUR MIND BE LIGHT.

WHAT WEIGHT ARE YOU CARRYING TODAY?

WHAT MIGHT YOU DO TO LEAVE IT BEHIND YOU?

WRITE A KIND MESSAGE TO YOURSELF BELOW:

FIND JOY IN MAKING SOMETHING TODAY.

Transform the dots below into flowers or
anything that comes to mind as you draw.

Write three things that you are good at making:

1.

2.

3.

Look to your dreams for insight.

THINK OF THE LAST DREAM YOU REMEMBER HAVING.
WHAT WAS IT ABOUT?

WHAT EMOTIONS DO YOU ASSOCIATE WITH THAT DREAM?

WHAT DO YOU WISH YOU COULD DREAM ABOUT TONIGHT?

LET YOUR MIND WANDER.
RECORD YOUR UNCENSORED STREAM OF
CONSCIOUSNESS BELOW. LET YOUR PEN FOLLOW
IN THE FOOTPRINTS OF YOUR THOUGHTS.

WRITE THE THINGS YOU CARE ABOUT TODAY
NEAR THE CENTER OF THE BULLSEYE.

WRITE THE THINGS YOU'RE GOING TO LET GO OF TODAY
ON THE OUTER RINGS OF THE BULLSEYE AND BEYOND.

USE SOUND AS A SIMPLE MEDITATION DEVICE.

Download a mindfulness bell or gong that reverberates loudly and play it as you sit quietly, focusing in on nothing but the sound. As the noise fades into oblivion, imagine that your stress is doing the same.

WHICH SOUNDS CALM YOU?

WHERE DID YOUR THOUGHTS GO AS YOU WAITED FOR THE SOUND TO DISSIPATE?

THE TIME TO RELAX
is when you don't have time for it.

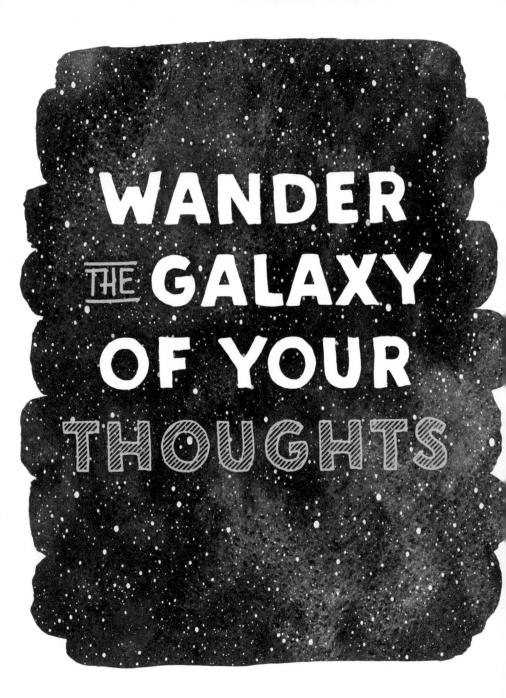

COLOR IN THE EMPTY GLASS BELOW
TO REFLECT HOW POSITIVE YOUR THOUGHTS ARE AT THE MOMENT:

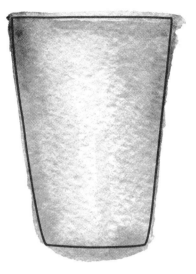

IF YOUR CUP ISN'T FULL, EXPLAIN WHY:

MAKE A POINT TO BE WOWED BY NATURE TODAY.

CATCH THE SUNRISE, MARVEL AT BIRDS IN FLIGHT, OR STEP OUTSIDE TONIGHT TO SEE THE BRILLIANT ARRANGEMENT OF STARS.

DESCRIBE OR DRAW WHAT YOU SEE HERE:

WHAT IN NATURE BRINGS YOU THE MOST COMFORT AND PEACE?

CHOOSE ONE THE ITEMS BELOW TO BE THE SYMBOL OF YOUR INNER PEACE. RETURN TO THIS IMAGE IN YOUR MIND AS A REMINDER TO SLOW DOWN OR RELAX.

THE OCEAN TIDE

THE SUN

SNOWFALL

DISTANT MOUNTAINS

BILLOWING CLOUDS

A GENTLE RAIN

WHAT JUDGMENTS (GOOD AND BAD) DO YOU
THINK PEOPLE MAKE ABOUT YOU?

CROSS OUT THE ONES THAT BOTHER YOU MOST.
WHY DO THEY BOTHER YOU?

Make some judgments about yourself below:

I AM A CARING...

I'M DOING THE BEST I CAN AT ...

MY STRENGTH IS MY...

I'M BECOMING A BETTER....

I SHOULD BE PROUD OF MYSELF FOR ...

MAKE
peace
WITH
YOURSELF

IF YOU COULD GIVE YOURSELF A GIFT TODAY, WHAT WOULD IT BE?

WHAT GIFTS ARE YOU LUCKY TO HAVE IN YOUR LIFE? COLOR IN THE WORDS THAT REPRESENT THEM:

HEALTH

FAMILY

LOVED ONES

OPPORTUNITY

SAFETY

PEACE OF MIND

HOME

EDUCATION

FRIENDS

ADD MORE HERE:

WRITE A PEP TALK FOR
WHEN YOU GET STUCK IN A RUT.

Remind yourself of what makes you truly happy
and how you can get back to it:

LET
HAPPINESS
FIND YOU

KITCHEN

CAREER PLAN

CHAOS IS BOTH NATURAL AND BEAUTIFUL.

What are some areas of your life or home that tend to get messy?

SOCK DRAWER

EX-BOYFRIEND
FEELINGS

car trunk

Star the item on this list that you try hardest to make sense of
or organize. Consider whether this item is meant to be chaotic.
If it is, fill in the permission slip to the right.

DATE:

TODAY I'M GIVING MYSELF PERMISSION TO STOP
FEELING BAD ABOUT THE STATE OF MY

....

IT WANTS TO BE MESSY. IT MIGHT EVEN NEED
TO BE MESSY.

I WILL STOP FIGHTING IT AND EMBRACE THE CHAOS.

SIGNED,

....

TAKE A LOAD OFF TODAY.
WHAT PRESSURES ARE YOU UNDER?
LIST THEM BELOW:

PRESSURES I PUT ON MYSELF ⬇

PRESSURES OTHERS PUT ON ME ⬇

FEEL THE WEIGHT OF ALL THOSE PRESSURES ON YOUR SHOULDERS.

NOW IMAGINE THE FEELING OF THAT WEIGHT SLOWLY LIFTING OFF YOU.
WHAT WOULD YOU BE FREE TO DO?

WRITE WHAT IT MEANS TO YOU TO BE A GOOD:

PERSON...

PARTNER...

PARENT...

IN WHICH ROLE DO YOU SHINE BRIGHTEST?

IN WHICH ROLE DO YOU STRUGGLE
MOST AND WHY?

ARE YOU BEING TOO HARD ON YOURSELF?
EXPLAIN.

Take a minute to lie or sit down for a simple meditation break.

USE YOUR BREATH TO NOTICE EACH PART OF YOU, STARTING WITH YOUR TOES. EVERY TIME YOU SLOWLY EXHALE, MOVE YOUR FOCUS UPWARD TO THE NEXT CHECKPOINT ON YOUR BODY.

WHERE DID YOU FEEL PLEASANT SENSATIONS
LIKE WARMTH OR RELAXATION?

WHERE DID YOU FEEL UNPLEASANT SENSATIONS
LIKE STRESS, TIGHTNESS, OR TENSION?

TENSION IS WHO YOU THINK YOU SHOULD BE.

Relaxation is who you are.

—CHINESE PROVERB

HOW WELL DO YOU HANDLE MAKING MISTAKES?

DOES THIS WORK FOR YOU OR DO YOU NEED A NEW APPROACH?

ALL OF THESE INVENTIONS
WERE MADE BY MISTAKE:

MICROWAVE
POST-IT NOTES
POTATO CHIPS
PLASTIC
STAINLESS STEEL
PLAY-DOH
SUPERGLUE

MAKE A POINT TO USE ONE OF THESE
ITEMS TODAY AS A REMINDER THAT
FAILURE CAN LEAD TO SUCCESS

WRITE DOWN 4 POSITIVE STATEMENTS ABOUT YOURSELF.

1.

2.

3.

4.

NOTICE WHETHER IT WAS EASY OR DIFFICULT
TO WRITE THOSE STATEMENTS.

If it was easy, write more! If it was difficult, write many more!

FIND MORE TO
LOVE ABOUT YOURSELF

Read the following:

LIFE IS NOT A TO-DO LIST. LIFE IS NOT A TO-DO LIST.
LIFE IS NOT A TO-DO LIST. LIFE IS NOT A TO-DO LIST.
LIFE IS NOT A TO-DO LIST. LIFE IS NOT A TO-DO LIST.
LIFE IS NOT A TO-DO LIST. LIFE IS NOT A TO-DO LIST.
LIFE IS NOT A TO-DO LIST. LIFE IS NOT A TO-DO LIST.
LIFE IS NOT A TO-DO LIST. LIFE IS NOT A TO-DO LIST.
LIFE IS NOT A TO-DO LIST. LIFE IS NOT A TO-DO LIST.
LIFE IS NOT A TO-DO LIST. LIFE IS NOT A TO-DO LIST.
LIFE IS NOT A TO-DO LIST. LIFE IS NOT A TO-DO LIST.
LIFE IS NOT A TO-DO LIST. LIFE IS NOT A TO-DO LIST.
LIFE IS NOT A TO-DO LIST. LIFE IS NOT A TO-DO LIST.
LIFE IS NOT A TO-DO LIST. LIFE IS NOT A TO-DO LIST.
LIFE IS NOT A TO-DO LIST. LIFE IS NOT A TO-DO LIST.
LIFE IS NOT A TO-DO LIST. LIFE IS NOT A TO-DO LIST.
LIFE IS NOT A TO-DO LIST. LIFE IS NOT A TO-DO LIST.
LIFE IS NOT A TO-DO LIST. LIFE IS NOT A TO-DO LIST.
LIFE IS NOT A TO-DO LIST. LIFE IS NOT A TO-DO LIST.
LIFE IS NOT A TO-DO LIST. LIFE IS NOT A TO-DO LIST.

What is life to you?

DEFINE IT HERE AS BEST AS YOU CAN AND RETURN TO THIS DEFINITION
WHEN YOU FEEL YOURSELF VEERING OFF TRACK.

DO YOU FEEL CONNECTED TO OTHERS TODAY, OR DISCONNECTED?

WHAT PEOPLE, PLACES, AND ACTIVITIES HELP YOU STAY CONNECTED?

WHAT PEOPLE, PLACES, AND ACTIVITIES MAKE YOU FEEL ISOLATED?

CONSIDER THE LAST TIME
YOU FELT DISCONNECTED:
ALONE ON AN ISLAND OF THOUGHTS AND
FEELINGS. HOW COULD YOU HAVE
"RESCUED" YOURSELF FROM THIS FEELING?
WHAT "MESSAGE" COULD YOU SEND TO
OTHERS FOR HELP? WRITE IT IN THE
BOTTLE BELOW.

WHAT ALWAYS AMAZES YOU?

Identify something below that sparks awe and appreciation in you, or scribble in your own source of wonder below:

a glowing fire

a lightning storm

a mountaintop view

a newborn baby

violin music

a bird's nest

Write a poem or ode to something that amazes you here:

CHALLENGE YOUR INNER CRITIC,

THAT VOICE THAT SAYS WHAT YOU'RE DOING IS NOT GOOD ENOUGH.
WHAT NEGATIVE MESSAGES, IF ANY, DO YOU HEAR
FROM YOUR INNER CRITIC?

WHICH MESSAGES ARE BASED IN SELF-DOUBT, FEAR, AND ANXIETY
RATHER THAN TRUTH? TRANSLATE THEM INTO MORE OBJECTIVE AND
TRUTHFUL STATEMENTS BELOW:

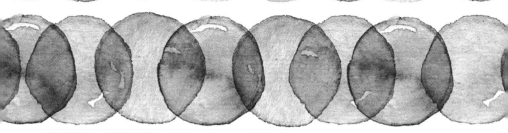

YOU'D NEVER ALLOW A PERSON TO TALK TO YOU
THE WAY YOUR INNER CRITIC DOES, RIGHT?

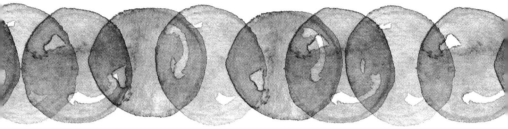

GET ANGRY AT IT. TELL THAT NASTY OGRE OF SELF-DOUBT
HOW WRONG IT REALLY IS:

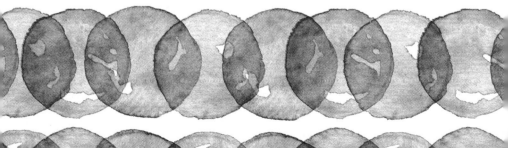

Write down all the things that are unique about you.

Return to this list when you feel that you are being too hard on yourself.

Beauty is a light in ꞏthe꞉ heart.

– Khalil Gibran

THINK OF THE PRESENT AS
THE SHORELINE IN THIS IMAGE.

WHAT 3 THINGS ARE YOU MOVING TOWARD IN YOUR FUTURE?

PICTURE THEM IN THE SKY ABOVE THE MOUNTAIN.

WHAT 3 THINGS ARE YOU LEAVING BEHIND IN YOUR PAST?

PICTURE THEM IN THE RIPPLING WATERS.

RUN YOUR FINGER SLOWLY FROM LEFT TO RIGHT ALONG
THE SHORELINE AND SAVOR THIS PRESENT MOMENT.

WHAT MOMENT TODAY WAS MOST JOYFUL?

WHAT DO YOU THINK MADE THIS MOMENT
SO JOYFUL?

HOW CAN YOU MAKE SPACE IN YOUR LIFE FOR
MORE OF THESE JOYFUL MOMENTS?

BE HAPPY
FOR THIS
MOMENT.

THIS
MOMENT IS
YOUR LIFE.

—OMAR KHAYYAM

Spend more time on your own today.

SIT WITH YOUR THOUGHTS AND RESIST THE URGE
TO DO ANY MORE THAN JUST THAT.

HOW COMFORTABLE ARE YOU BEING ALONE FOR MOST OF A DAY?

WHAT FEELINGS ARISE WHEN YOU
SPEND A LOT OF TIME ALONE?

Loneliness is
THE POVERTY OF SELF:

Solitude is
THE RICHNESS OF SELF.

—May Sarton

RUNNING GARDENING

WHAT HABIT COULD YOU START PRACTICING IN ORDER TO BE MORE PRESENT?

reading

DRAWING

WHAT DISTRACTIONS COULD BE REMOVED FROM YOUR DAILY LIFE?

HOW COULD YOU MAKE YOUR HOME A MORE PEACEFUL OR MINDFUL PLACE?

Color this mandala while you think of ideas.

RIVERS KNOW THIS:

THERE IS NO HURRY. WE SHALL GET THERE SOME DAY.

—A.A. MILNE

WHAT EXPERIENCES ARE YOU GRATEFUL
TO HAVE BEHIND YOU?

WHAT EXPERIENCES ARE YOU GLAD
TO HAVE AHEAD OF YOU?

WHAT DO YOU WISH WOULD NEVER CHANGE?

HOW MIGHT IT CHANGE IN A WAY THAT ADDS
UNEXPECTED JOY TO YOUR LIFE?

LOOK FOR INSPIRATION TODAY.

Whether it's a new song, a quote that rouses your spirit,
a person who exhibits strength, or a glorious piece of architecture,
seek it out. Write about things that inspire you here:

HOW CAN YOU ADD MORE INSPIRING ELEMENTS
LIKE THIS TO YOUR LIFE?

DESCRIBED HOW LOVED
YOU FEEL RIGHT NOW.

HOW CAN YOU ADD MORE LOVE
TO YOUR LIFE OR THE LIVES OF OTHERS?

WHAT ABOUT LOVE ISN'T PERFECT?

WHAT LIFE LOVES ARE YOU
GRATEFUL TO HAVE EXPERIENCED?

*Your flaws are proof that you're human.
Next time you feel the need to fix them,
give them a friendly nod instead.*

WHAT DO YOU PERCEIVE TO BE YOUR STRENGTHS?

WHAT DO YOU PERCEIVE TO BE YOUR FLAWS?

IN WHAT WAY ARE YOUR FLAWS ENDEARING?
WHO DOESN'T SEEM TO MIND THEM AT ALL?

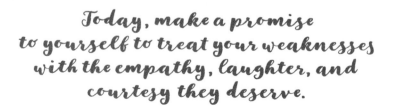

Today, make a promise
to yourself to treat your weaknesses
with the empathy, laughter, and
courtesy they deserve.

DESCRIBE YOUR LIFE AS AN OUTSIDER LOOKING IN.

WHAT DO YOU THINK SOMEONE MIGHT ENVY
ABOUT YOUR LIFE?

THE SECRET TO HAVING IT ALL IS KNOWING

that you already do.

WHAT WEATHER IS BREWING INSIDE YOU TODAY?
Take stock of your emotions by placing a hand gently
on your heart and taking several deep breaths.
Write how you feel below:

ARE YOUR EMOTIONS GUIDING YOU TODAY OR GETTING IN YOUR WAY?

Color in this bar graph to see how you're truly feeling:

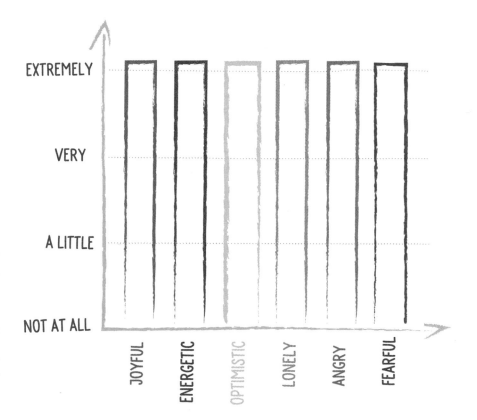

Being present in the moment means considering how you're feeling, even in the most heated of moments.

WHAT ELICITS A STRONG NEGATIVE REACTION IN YOU?

DESCRIBE YOUR BODY IN THESE MOMENTS
(HEART RACING, STOMACH DROPPING, HEAD THROBBING, ETC.):

WHAT DO YOU THINK IS THE REAL REASON FOR THIS REACTION?

WRITE A CAUSE
IN THE RED CIRCLE
ON THE LEFT.

WRITE THE UNWANTED
EFFECT IN THE
YELLOW CIRCLE
ON THE RIGHT.

WRITE THE PHRASE
'WILLING PAUSE' BETWEEN THE TWO CIRCLES
AND RETRACE THE WORDS SEVERAL TIMES.

SOMETIMES A FEW MOMENTS OF SELF-AWARENESS
CAN HOLD BACK THE STORM OF YOUR EMOTIONS
AND HELP YOU LET GO.

WHAT ARE SOME PRESSURES (INTERNAL OR EXTERNAL)
FROM WHICH YOU'RE **READY TO FREE YOURSELF?**

WHAT HELPS YOU **BE MORE PRESENT** IN YOUR LIFE?

WHAT IS THE BEST THING YOU CAN THINK OF
TO WRITE ABOUT YOURSELF RIGHT NOW? **MAKE IT GOOD!**
HERE ARE SOME SUGGESTIONS...

I've always been true to myself.

I've always been good enough.

I deserve all the happiness I get.

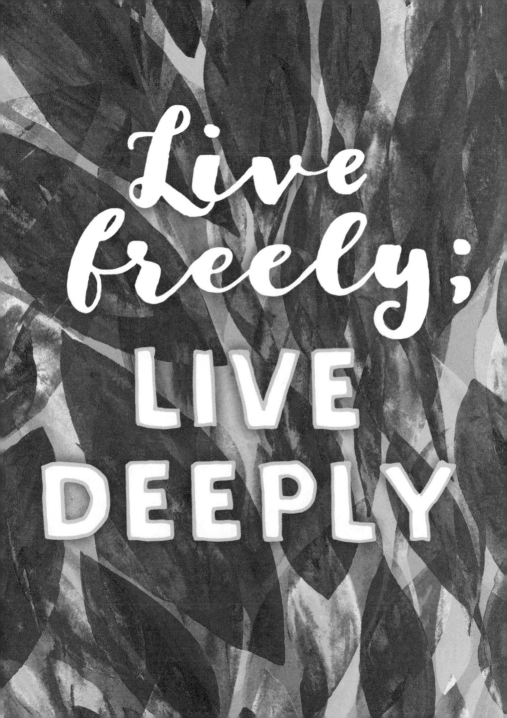

WE LIVE IN DEEDS,
NOT YEARS;
IN THOUGHTS,
NOT BREATHS;

IN FEELINGS,
NOT IN FIGURES
ON A DIAL.

WE SHOULD COUNT TIME
BY HEART-THROBS.

—FROM *FESTUS: A POEM*, BY PHILIP JAMES BAILEY

FILL THIS PAGE WITH A COLLECTION
OF HEART-THROB MOMENTS AND RESOLVE TO COLLECT MORE.

ACKNOWLEDGMENTS

SPECIAL THANKS TO **THERESA WIGGINS, M.ED.**
OF VILLAGE PARENTING FOR HER LESSONS IN MINDFULNESS.